TRAILING YOU

TRAILING YOU

poems by

Kimberly M. Blaeser

TRAILING YOU
Poems by Kimberly M. Blaeser

Copyright 1994 by Kimberly M. Blaeser

ISBN 0-912678-88-7

Library of Congress #94-75714

Cover art: Songmaker by Charles B. Mitchell

Design and composition of cover and text by Sans Serif Inc., Ann Arbor, MI

The Greenfield Review Press
Greenfield Center, New York 12833

Distributed by The Talman Company, Inc.
131 Spring St.
New York, NY 10012

for the Blaesers, Bunkers and Antells
for you who carry those names in your blood
for you who carry those names in your spirits

Contents

IV
Road Show

V
Sewing Memories

Acknowledgments

Migwetch to my family and the many friends who have supported me in my writing. Thanks to the "Returning the Gift" project, responsible for fostering inspiration and connections between the web of native writers. Special thanks to past and present members of "Word Warriors" for thoughtful and considerate readings of my works-in-progress.

Grateful acknowledgement is also made to the editors of the following publications in which some of these poems first appeared: *Nebraska English Journal*: "Rituals, Yours–and Mine," "Downwinders," and "Surviving Winter." *Unsettling America: Race and Ethnicity in Contemporary American Poetry*: "Certificate of Live Birth." *Dreams and Secrets*: "Trailing You." *Akwe:kon Journal*: "Road Show," and "Trailing You." *The Colour of Resistance*: "Living History," "Certificate of Live Birth: Escape From the Third Dimension," "Sewing Memories." *Northeast Indian Quarterly*, "On the Way to the Chicago Pow-Wow." *Loonfeather*: "Living History," "Asphalt the Odd Perfume of Summer," "On the Way to the Chicago Pow-Wow," and "Alaskan Mountain Poems: Transfiguration." *Gatherings: The En'owkwin Journal of First North American Peoples, Volume IV, Re-Generation: Expanding the Web to Claim the Future*: "Speaking Those Names," and "Ice Tricksters and Shadow Stories." *Gatherings: The En'owkwin Journal of First North American Peoples, Volume III, Mother Earth Perspectives: Preservation Through Words*: "Where I Was That Day." *Studies in American Indian Literature*: "Trailing You." *Returning the Gift*: "Native Americans vs. The Poets," "Where I Was That Day," "Living History," "Trailing You."

Preface

Harold Bloom wrote of the "anxiety of influence." I offer these poems instead as a celebration of influence. Claiming or believing in an individual voice, we delude ourselves. No voice arises from one person. I know that I write out of a place, a center, that is greater than what I alone am or could be. My work is filled with the voices of other people. It crosses boundaries of time and space, of ways of knowing, of what it means to be human. Like a dream, it visits or is visited by the people, places, stories, and events that shadow and shape my present. I think the act of writing itself is a quest, a way of discovering where we stand in relationship to all else. Therefore, my writing becomes an act that re-creates me.

Much of my life and my writing searches out the connections of self, family, community, place and history. Like many Indian people, I write partly to remember, because remembering, we recover; remembering, we survive. I think the best poems might be nothing more than a list of names of people, animals, places, plants, sounds, seasons, because poetry is connections and these are the connections—the poetry—we all carry in our soul, the poetry that writers try to bring to the surface.

These poems I write for Twin Lakers who remember Bass Lake, Sargent Lake, Naytahwaush, B.A.B., lonesome pine, the hollow, Ike Antell, Maymie Bunker, Shelly Turner, Selam Ross, choke-cherries, cranberries, hazelnuts, milkweed, smartweed, wiigob, fry bread, waabooz, manoomin, fried oatmeal, outhouses, slop pails, hauling water, mending nets, the sugarbush, Olson's landing, the corner store, Peppy, Sig'um, Larkie, Beasty. . . .

I

Living History

Speaking Those Names

aloud
speaking those names
you have given me
calling myself by those names
in just that voice that you have spoken
hearing myself in those names
each time
I become again myself
my holding-your-hand self
my hair braided, round cheeked self
my barefoot, fringed cut-off self
my lace tights, Easter hat self,
my watermelon loving, woodtick hating self,
my child self, my teen-age self, my now self
my whole self
I hear myself in those names
being pulled back by those names
know again myself in relationship

aloud
mustoord
kim-a-dill
lady
tim-ber-ly
speaking them out loud in rescue
hearing them out loud in your voice
mine sunshine
you can answer some of these kimbee
come on my girl
knowing by those names who I was

to you
to myself
becoming again those names
sister
white head
the brain
mimmie
being claimed again in names
spoken then
named across time
k-k
across death
kimmie
across change
dr.
hearing you call
kiii-iiimmm
claiming myself
in speaking those names
aloud

Living History

Walked into Pinehurst, sunburned, smelling of fish,
Big Indian man paying for some gas and a six pack,
Looking at me hard.
Dreamer, I think. Too old for me.
Heads right toward me.
"Jeez," he says, "You look just like your mom-
You must be Marlene's girl."
Pinches my arm, but I guess it's yours
he touches.
Hell, wasn't even looking at me.
Wonder if I'm what they call living history?

History Again

I.

You know the story:
John Muir punctures his eye
aqueous humors drip into his cupped hand
ten minutes later the sight is gone.
In sympathy or hystericism the second eye loses sight—
He is blind.
Three months of darkness.

But the light returned
and Muir was changed:
Found Alaska, found the Sierra Mountains, found himself
a naturalist fighting for wilderness preservation,
alive at the top of a tree in an electrical storm,
alive behind the wall of rushing water at Yosemite Falls,
living now not getting a living.

II.

At Yosemite clinic
just down from Muir's Hetch Hetchy
waiting to have my punctured eye treated
Ironic? Symbolic? My subconscious at work?
My John Muir imitation . . .
If only I could grow a beard, pack my knapsack,
put on my hiking boots, live on good bread and tea,
If only I could walk backwards
into history
If only I could find the light to change my life, too.

Ice Tricksters and Shadow Stories

for Jerry

I.

Later that winter she began to hear voices.
No insistent whispers of conscience,
Not the teasing of her muse,
Voices of ice, ice voices.
Tinkling like wind chimes,
    the coated branches of trees,
Waking her again at night,
    banging and booming across the wide expanse of frozen lake.
Ice, a delicate porcelain,
    shattering with a hollow pop beneath her feet;
Screeching beneath the sled runners,
    mock pain echoing in winter silence.

II.

Her companions all deaf to the diamond poetry of ice
She, fearing the beauty, the coming of this new ice age,
Listened in trembling search to sounds become voices
Become words become shadow stories of ice.
Recalling the mystery of ice point,
    the temperature of equilibrium of pure water and ice;
Remembering the story, how ice woman froze the wiindigoo
    at just that point in the moccasin game.
Having sought herself that delicate equilibrium
    between recklessness and cowering,
Knowing truly how the balance of story sustains two natures,
    she began to imagine, ice shadows.

For Africa's ice plant, a trickster story:
  fleshy leaves covered with glistening crystals,
A suspended transformation, a metaphor for life,
  like the evil gambler frozen by ancient ice woman,
Like delicate ice needles, floating in midair,
  finding the circumstances to defy gravity.
Suspended herself, frozen in winter time, an ice floe
  locked happily in a glacial epoch,
Sustained now by the hypnotic voices of ice—
  trickling, tinkling, cracking, booming
Ice tricksters telling story
She began to hear.

III.

Hearing, too, at last,
  their sounding the metaphors of death,
In the trees, limbs enveloped in glitter,
On the ledge, spikes honed of crystal water,
Both incandescent, resplendent with their sun death
Ice capsules weeping their own doom, icicles crashing to earth.
Angry now, she skated madly by the moon's light,
Feigning indifference, ignoring the screaming sound
When her blades cut a fresh path across the hardened lake,
Believing somehow she was forestalling breakup, meltdown, spring,
Knowing human things like refrigeration and dry ice,
Believing in the science of Celsius and centigrade,
Thinking ice trickster to be of water and winter,
Subject to simple laws of time and temperature,
Forgetting temporarily the ice shadows cast by myth.

8

IV.

Then falling one night asleep or beneath the ice,
Finding herself pulled from dream or watery death,
To waken damp with memories of a silent ice woman.
Wondering had she been rescued or been condemned,
Wondering if she was human, or ice, or shadow,
Wondering if her voice sounded or was silent,
Wondering if her story was the present or the past,
Wondering if she was myth or reality,
Wondering finally, if perhaps they weren't the same,
At least the same, in that mysterious center,
    that ice point of consciousness,
    that place of timeless equilibrium
    where one begins at last to understand voices.

Don't Send Me Any Surveys

If you asked me what color is the sunset
I could not answer you
Because the sunset is alive and changing
As I am too
You ask me do I believe A, B, or C
And I can't answer you
Because I believe what the sunset tells me
And it tells me something new each day
Don't send me any surveys

You grow impatient with me
when I ask you what the questions mean
They are obvious, completely objective,
require no thought you say
I wonder to myself why you ask them then
but I try to be cooperative

You ask me where I was born and where I live
And I can't answer you
Because I am a part of the life that has ever been
That lives in the trees and the earth and the air
The same life that was born in my grandmother and mother and
    now in me
You ask me then how old I am 12–18, 19–26, 27–35, 36–42. . .
How can I answer that
When I am so old and so young at the same time?

If you asked a butterfly its age
would she be as old as the larvae from which she came?
the age of the caterpillar that crawls about?
as old as the cocoon tucked under the leaf of the lilac bush?
or as young as the butterfly that flits about the summer flower?
Until you learn to understand the questions
Don't send me any surveys

On the Way to the Chicago Pow-Wow

On the way to the Chicago pow-wow,
Weaving through four-lanes of traffic,
   going into the heart of Carl Sandburg's hog-butcher to the world,
   ironic, I think, landing at Navy Pier for a pow-wow.
I think of what Roberta said: "Indian people across the country
   are working on a puzzle, trying to figure out what I call
   –the abyss."
Driving into the abyss. Going to a pow-wow.

On the way to the Chicago pow-wow,
Laugh when I look down at my hands.
Trying to tell you, needing to hear you laugh out loud
   because the puzzle was made by madmen who want us all lost
   in the rotating maze.
I think my hands have stepped out of Linda Hogan's poem:
One wears silver and tourquoise, a Zuni bracelet and a Navaho ring.
One wears gold and diamonds, an Elgin watch and a Simonson's
   half-carat;
The madman's classic mixedblood, a cliche.
Together, laughing out loud at the madness. Going to a
pow-wow.

On the way to the Chicago pow-wow,
Thinking of home, I know we are driving the wrong way.
It's not Lake Michigan I want to see.
It's not Wriggly Field.
But there is no exit here to 113, no cut-across.

I think of Helen's cabin, sitting by the fire drying my hair,
  and Collin talking:
  "Sometimes you have to go in the wrong direction
  to get where you're heading."
Driving southeast, heading northwest. Heading home,
  to White Earth Lake,
  to Indian ball diamonds,
  to open air pow-wows.
Taking the Eden's, going to the Chicago pow-wow,
  on the way back home.

Rituals, Yours — and Mine

I.

living by your words
as if i haven't enough of my own
ever
to make them stretch
that long distance
from home to here
from then to now

and all the new words
i've ever read learned
or shelved so neatly
can't explain myself to me
like yours always do

sometimes that one gesture
of your chin and lips
my memory of
the sideways movement of your eyes
are the only words
from that language
i can manage
to put things in their place

II.

walked in on you today
closed the screened door quietly
so you wouldn't notice

just yet
stood watched you
mumbling shuffling about the kitchen
your long yellow-gray braid
hanging heavy down your back

wanted to see you turn
just that way
hear that familiar exclamation
you snapping the dishtowel
landing it just short of me
shame on me for surprising you

you walk toward me laughing
don't change anything I chant silently
wiping your hands on your faded print apron
you lay them gently still damp cool
one on each side of my face
for that long long second

"When'd you come? Sit down, I'm making breakfast."
I watch the wrinkled loose flesh jiggle on your arms
as you reach to wind and pin your braid
hurry to find your teeth behind the water pail
pull up your peanut butter stockings
pull down your flowered house dress
and wet your fingers
to smooth the hair back behind your ears

III.

smoothing away time with the fluid line
of your memory
I am in place at your table
in the morning damp of your still dark kitchen
I wait for you to come

stepping through the curtained doorway
you enter intent on this day
restart the fire
fill place the kettle
pull open the kitchen door
inviting daylight to come
welcoming it into your house—
bringing it into mine.

II

Where I was that Day

Where I Was That Day

It wasn't just the pill bugs
gray, many-legged and pulling that stunt
like they always did
closing in on themselves
contracting into the tiny round mass
like an image of the origin circle
And it wasn't the turtle alone either
who became so neatly one half of the earth's sphere

It was partly that day when I stopped at the little creek
and noticed the funny bumps on that floating log
and how they seemed to be looking at me
and how they were really little heads with beady bulging eyes
and how when I came back a half an hour later
the bumps had been rearranged on that log

It was partly the butterflies that would materialize
out of the flower blossoms
and the deer that appeared and disappeared into the forest
while standing stalk still
whose shape would be invisible one minute
and would stand out clearly the next
like the image in one of the connect-the-dot puzzles

It was the stick bugs, the chameleon
the snakes that became branches
the opossum who was dead then suddenly alive
And it was me who fit and saw one minute so clearly
and then stumbled blind the next
that made me think we are all always finding our place

in the great sphere of creation
that made me know I could learn a way
to pull the world around me too
to color myself with earth and air and water
and so become indistinguishable
to match my breath to the one
to pulse in and out with the mystery
to be both still and wildly alive in the same moment
to be strangely absent from myself
and yet feel large as all creation
to know
to know
to know and to belong
while the spell holds
learning to hold it a little longer each time

That's where I was that day
I watched you from the arbor
never blinking
while you looked all about for me
and then turned back home
thinking to find me in another place
when I was there everywhere you looked
I knew then the stories about Geronimo were true
and that he did turn to stone
while the cavalries passed him by
mistook him for just a part of the mountain
when he had really become the whole mountain
and all the air they breathed
and even the dust beneath their horse's hooves

I walk about trying to find the place I was that day
but getting there seems harder now
I feel heavier, my spirit weighted down
and I'm thinking I must shed something
like the animals shed their hair or skin

lose even their antlers annually
while I hold on to everything
and I'm thinking I must change my colors
like the rabbit, the ptarmigan, the weasel
and I'm thinking I must spin a cocoon
grow wings and learn to fly
and I'm thinking I must hibernate and fast
feed off my own excess for a season
and then perhaps emerge
in the place I was that day
and stay there longer this time

And I walk about and watch the creatures
the tree toads becoming and unbecoming a part of the trunk
the rocks in my path that crack open into grasshoppers and fly away
the spider who hangs suspended before me
and then disappears into thin air
and I feel comforted
knowing we are all
in this puzzle together
knowing we are all just learning
to hold the spell
a little longer
each time

In the Cold Rain Walking

I.

I tell myself the rain came suddenly today
Only the dog and I know
we brought it on ourselves
Walking out, far, beyond shelter
We saw the lone dark threatening cloud
Felt the wind chill all about us
"What do you think, Tawn?"
Her tail takes refuge between her legs
She thinks humans have no sense
"You don't mind getting a little wet, do you?"
I know she minds, but I want to stay out just now
One are-you-crazy look for the record and she gives in
We go on ears and hair blowing out behind us
Dampness brings each aroma close to taste
The drops begin large and cold but sparse
their rhythm picks up
soon they are pulsing fast against my skin
cold water running of my face and hair
my clothes stuck tightly to my body
streams of water making their way down my bare legs
my shoes squishing now with each step

II.

In the cold rain walking heavily
Memories wash over me like the rain
Yesterday's waters wash over me again
We wear heavy water-soaked tennis shoes with our swimsuits

when we suspect the lake bottom may be littered with trash
or the rocks covered with slippery weeds and algae
We jump in fully clothed whenever we feel the urge
We swim in the rain, we ride the waves of the high winds
We watch while the little minnows hover about our legs
tickling us trying to bite us we think
We hold our breath, stand on our heads, float on our backs
twirl madly about on our inner tubes
till the world of the shore is distant, gone out of focus
We swim in the noonday sun, we swim at midnight,
we swim in the early spring when ice still lines the shores
we swim in the hottest dog-days of august
we swim across the narrows of Bass Lake and back
we swim out beyond time
somewhere
having water fights
playing tag
flipping each other with joined hands
high into the air
splashing loudly
diving deeply
skimming the bottom too closely sometimes
we swim

III.

In the cold rain walking on through time
Seeing myself at sixteen on that county highway
Hitchhiking with you to see your boyfriend
Standing in the rain trying to describe the way we looked
"Desolate," you said but we weren't then
Laughing through everything the way we could together
Being young and sure friends could be trusted
Seeing myself at twelve taking shelter under that tarp
Huddled without fear against the storm

Talking about the way the fish began biting with the rain
Hearing you say they always did like a little rain
Getting warm and dried out by the fire
Feeling happy, the four of us, huddled there together
Wanting to tell the boat that came to rescue us
To go away, leave us in peace, but all having to be polite
and pretend to be thankful to be taken back into the cold rain
Seeing myself at eighteen using the rain to wash my car
Trying to get you to stay out and play in the rain, too
Seeing you watch me from the window across the street
Knowing you wanted to abandon adulthood then
just for a little while like I do now
thinking of you telling me later you wished you'd stayed
promising myself then I would always choose to stay
knowing that I haven't always but did today anyway

IV.

In the cold rain walking swiftly now remembering
The pileated woodpecker whose loud tapping called the storm
that Boundary Waters' morning
the sky shape carved and colored so beautifully
we stood on the rock cliffs and watched it come
until we had time enough only to grab the lightest things
and run with them to the tent shelter
With such force that woodpecker storm blew
we watched our cooking pans scattered here and there
sat inside as our tiny tent ballooned its stakes pulled loose
holding it down at the corners with our bodies
laughing we feared and hoped that we might be lifted
and carried off in those woodpecker winds
be against all causes made to soar
lifted beyond ourselves on woodpecker winds
in the storm in the rain calling for it then
tapping that storm into and out of time

24

V.

After the cold rain walking returning here
Stopping to taste the still wet red raspberries
Made sweeter by the rain like we

Sleeping With McKenzie

Flaunting
taut flesh
leanness

Sensuous yawning
swanning neck
pink tongue
the stretch you take
preparing yourself

Watching your sleekness
McKenzie
curving, turning, hunting
finding that perfect
elusive space
on the border of wakefulness

Settling yourself
against me
head
heavy
on the curve
at my waist

I've waited, McKenzie
this moment

Teach me
how
to drop
earthly burdens
to move with you

So gently
into
that floating web where dreams reside

McKenzie
tiger songs
rock against your throat
vibrations
caresses of sound

May I?
sink with you
into animal oblivion

Will you?
sing me there
with
breathy purring

who takes me places where poems live

who says that poetry is difficult
except for the sound
which he can understand as music

who wonders where the ideas come from
that write themselves into lines
late at night while he sits watch

who'd rather read a newspaper than a novel
because he hasn't a taste for stories
who when we chase the day about
in rain returning cold and hungry
carries back soggy sounds and images
drying them out with me before a fire
as if they weren't the very fabric of story

who tells me what the news is
and what the names of things are
and how the world got to be the way
we wish together it wasn't
who draws me maps I can follow
and reassures me into and out of cities

who takes me to swamps and ponds and streams
and creeks and lakes and all places of water
where words begin
to mountains, moraines and palisades
such places of height
where vision is born
to forests and meadows and gardens and thickets
to company with growing things

to ditches, kettles, valleys, gorges and canyons
each low lying place
where thoughts grow deeply
to homes of caribou, otter, moose, and shrews
ducks, cranes, eagles, jays and loons
where all voices sound

who takes me to weddings and funerals and family reunions
where the weak draw patterns and the brave relationships
to libraries and bookstores and chinese restaurants
to board meetings and back doctors
into the rush and into the hush
on boats and bikes, planes, trains, wagons and skis

who says he doesn't see how this leaves time
for poetry at all
as if all this were not the very stuff itself
as if he weren't
he—who takes me places where poems live.

Alaskan Mountain Stories, Transfiguration

I.

For months I planned to be mauled or eaten by the first grizzly that crossed my path. Late at night I lay wondering what to leave behind: labeled keys, letters, a will—just in case.

But I guess the grizzly had more important things to occupy his time. Or anyway, a better meal in mind than one scrawny mixed-blooded woman whose taste would have been spoiled anyway by the smell of fear.

Because, for all my preoccupation with my imminent death, he didn't as much as glance my way or even bother with my spoiled scent. As for me, I even faded from my own mind once in the presence of the bear.

I guess I was destroyed, after all, but in a much more useful way: Migwetch.

II.

How can I make these words sing for you the song I saw: that great blonde bear lumbering across the August tundra. . . This song has no sound, but only motion sending the words through the air.

Once forever the bear walked and ran on all fours. Mounds of flesh beneath his fur rippled and shook out the voice of motion. Tussocks shrank beneath his enormous paws and water splashed up onto his great hairy legs. He paused, rotated his neck to trace with his muzzle a half circle of air. And the globe moved a little on its axis.

Birds lighted round to watch him eat, to learn his song, to see him paw the air in gesture, point with his mouth – the tribal way – to a place beyond our visioning. At length the brush beside the creek opened up to welcome the singer there and then closed again behind him. Branches still sang the motion for a spell, but then the notes faded out.

And words and sound returned to the tundra.

learning, at last

I.

drops of morning dew
shimmering on fallen leaf

makes me wonder why
we cover ourselves at night

II.

drops of morning dew
renewing waters of life

making plans to leave
my spirit outside tonight

This Cocoon

I.

Fluttering
against my palm,
pollened wings.

Quick life,
pulsing
in my hand.

A feather tickle,
answered
by my flying heart
my child's glee
my hand's impulsive
frantic opening—
too soon.

You fly.

Again,
encircling you.
Cocoon
spun of flesh.
Winged vibrations
surprising me again.

Tingling,
a child of secrets.
Must not tell.

I ask
forgive me
and give me leave.
Share this portion
of butterfly life,
Let me
tap
your joy,
break out
for a moment
with wings.

We fly.

II.

Butterflies.
Ride my thoughts.

Three butterflies
have lighted
affixed themselves
like pinions
to my left shoulder.

I am winged.
Struck with awe.

Butterfly,

has my life glowed
sweet as yours?
that you have come
to feel
human flutter?

34

In this gift
or enchantment
I am captured.
Seek not
to win release.
Held fast
by butterfly feet.

From this cocoon
ta k e f l i g h t

Leaving Santa Fe

A bear,
a red-clay-colored bear
stalking across the land below.
Perhaps a shadow bear,
I think:
his shape secret
hidden to the eye at ground level.
His shadow stories
arrive that way
begin again
to tell themselves.
These are the stories I will need
to find my way
across the land
without
a red-clay-colored bear
inlayed.

III

Trailing You

Trailing You

for Ike

Trailing you in stories
and then in the dreams
that come just before morning
so that I wake listening for you to finish
what you were saying
or I sit up, swinging my legs to the side of the bed
rushing until my feet feel the carpet
and the rest of what I was expecting
becomes a dream too.
Those mornings I won't talk until
I go over it all slowly the way I remember it
waking up because my nose is so cold
and the fire has gone out in the bedroom stove
lying under the crazy quilt
peeking out of the blankets that cover the window to see
who is out in the yard
what kind of day it is
what's hanging on the clothesline
feeling the last warmth of the flannel sheets
before I swing my legs out and my bare feet touch
not carpet
but ice cold linoleum covered with bits of gritty sand
that stick to my feet
as I run into the kitchen
where a fire is going in the cook stove
where you have been sitting drinking coffee.
Sometimes I see your face when you turn
other times it won't come clear

but I refuse to look at the pictures
I want you more real than that
not to cry over as if you aren't still here.
If I could tell you the things I'm doing
bring them to you over smoked fish and coffee
you'd make them over for me with your talk and teasing
link with your eyes my past and present.
So I trail you waking and sleeping
hear you laughing as you splash cold water on my face
when I've slept too long
see your hands and hear the water
trickle into the wash basin as you pour for me
smell the side pork and hot biscuits
listen to you call "Kim-a-dill, Kim-a-dill"
as if I were a bird
and in these memories and dreams and stories of you
I find the places you sat and rested while cutting wood
I see the hole you broke in the ice when you fell through
and the path of broken ice as you kept heaving yourself up
over and over with your gun ahead of you all the way to shore
and I wonder if these poems are the path I make and I wonder
how far it is
to shore.

Surviving Winter
or
Old Stories We Tell Ourselves When a Blizzard is Coming

I.

About the three friends trapped for two days
when their car was buried in snow
and how they kept their hands and feet from freezing
by placing them in one another's arm pits

About the young boy on the snowmobile
whose engine died and left him stranded
when the wind chill was sixty below
and how he remembered what he had been told
about using nature for survival
and so built a snow cave
which insulated him from the winter wind
and thus made an ally of the cold snow

About the little girl who was playing in a snow tunnel
who when entering from the top
got stuck upside-down
with just her legs sticking out
and how she prayed and had faith
and believed even as she was passing out
that she would survive
and how she made herself visible to that one car
against the barren winter landscape
so that they had to notice what didn't fit

and so came to her rescue
and set her directions right again

And about that frozen lady from Lengby
who proved that antifreeze isn't just for cars
and how she became an excuse for all those
who wanted just one more for the road
one more bracer against the cold
to keep their vital organs going
even if their body might get stiff from the cold

And about our friend who knew that
taking supplies just in case
was easier if you carried the food in a full stomach
and that taking precautions
really meant having a bottle in a brown paper sack

And all the other winter stories that
teach us things we should know about survival
like about tying ropes to follow from the barn to the house
even though we think we could never get lost
because we walk that way every day
and about always carrying matches and that little candle
because its tiny spark of heat might be all we need to stay alive
and about not being too proud or too stupid
to drink the urine that is offered you
if that will keep you alive

II.

I used to think we told these stories
to learn to survive winter
but now I know that winter comes
so that we tell stories
and learn to survive life.

Frankie's Reign

I.

At three,
Deer dancing
magic through the kitchen.
Imagination claiming the world whole
My Santa Fe house
my mountains, arroyos
rainbows, cereal box toys
my pow-wow music.
Sitting with Hosteen
the wicker chair your throne
legs sticking straight out
too short to even dangle
you command each day.
Insisting on my hand when we walk
my lap my food my full attention
coaxing it from me with your
lilting call
running the vowel of my name up and down the scales
of your little boy voice
Kiiii-iiiim
I forget to be embarrassed as I twirl you in dance
at grownup dinner parties
smile even as I eat crumpled chocolate cookies
melting warm from your hand
We crouch together under the troll bridge
in the safe sweet world of our invention.

II.

At four,
little hands that labor
over Indian dolls
and castle puzzles
become an omen
of a story
no one wants to tell.
Who could believe the betrayal
of genes
in a world where little boys
lift high their knees
in deer dance magic.

III.

At five, at ten, at twenty,
I claim the world whole
for you
my imagination
my invention
your world, still.

p.s. write soon

I open my envelopes carefully, unsticking them at the flap;
I watch you slit yours at the seam
And toss some unopened into the garbage.
Sometimes when you watch I feign nonchalance,
But still I expect something
Not Ed McMann's millions, but something.
I've tried to get used to the convenience
Of a letter opener
I've tried to throw things without reading them,
But I'm always afraid I'll miss something
A message hidden under the flap
A kiss promised by the adolescent SWAK
Something, a word, a scent, a presence sealed in,
    waiting under the flap like dreams that stir beneath our waking.
In summer I sit outside with the animals
playing or resting in the sun
waiting for the mail to come
When it does I shuffle through it
Sometimes finding a letter or a package or an invitation
That makes me happy or excited
But never finding–it,
that thing that used to come in the mail
when I was five, six, seven, even ten
and my father used to write from Montana
and my Grandma and Auntie used to write from Minnesota
and my Uncle used to send me that ugly Indian doll every year
and my kindergarten teacher used to send presents in the summer
never finding that thing that came with secret-pal letters

that came even with the ring from the boy who I didn't think was
   anything so special until he sent it and I knew he thought I was
never finding that thing that came
with the first love letters I ever got
the one with evergreen needles in it
the one that came in French which I could only half decipher
the one that came special delivery
Sometimes I think it must be the postal service
I tell myself all my good mail
has ended up at the dead letter office in Washington, D. C.
So lately I've started listening for the phone,
You know I never could just let it ring without answering. . .

Two Haiku

I.

Watching the fireflies
Wishing I could see your eyes
Exploding with light

II.

Nighttime horizon
Heat lightning, fireflies, your eyes
Exploding distance

Dear Robert,

Fall scents arrived this morning as if by overnight mail.
I know you would say it smells like deer hunting,
but I smell something better than the days that came
when you had grown old enough
to go in the woods will all the other men,
when I was left behind
to cook and gossip with all the other women.
I smell that year when we were both on the brink of being too old,
too old to run in the woods in a game of chase
from early morning when the leaves were still damp
until early evening when woodsmoke from neighboring houses began
    to fill the air.
I still feel the ache of urgency of that year
when we ran as children for what we knew must be the last time,
before those big big woods shrunk
and the deep hollow became just a small dip.
It was time that filled in all the space of youth,
making everything smaller and closer together,
making things easier to reach but less worth the trouble.
But days like today and days of early spring too
all my world grows large again
and though now I walk through it
in my deepest feeling parts I run
and bury myself in the leaves
and push you in the wheelbarrow
and watch you whittle a branch you have cut
and try again to toss a knife like you have shown me
so that it lands stuck deeply in the ground.
I still know the contentment

of sitting in the sun on the bank of the river
while you cast out again and again
and reel in slowly each time
I watch the fish follow your lure
and I feel you are reeling me in that way too –
but I don't mind.
I know that feeling of perfect safety
as I follow you on my bike
and you call directions over your shoulder
and then look back to make sure I can
   climb the hill
     make the turn
         pedal through the gravel.
And then we arrive
and you show me that new place you have discovered
that you wanted me to see too
that place I would never have found on my own
would never have dared to travel to without you to follow.
But as the weeks pass I learn to go alone
and I rush to tell you
because I know you will be surprised
and then decide to take me to another even better place
on another path that only you could have charted.
And all our years go on like that
and so when fall comes suddenly in a moment
when March winds stop to let in the scent of spring
when the rivers and lakes are frozen just enough to venture out
when drowned angle worms cover the sidewalks
when fireflies flit over the cornfields
I feel your presence and your absence in the same moment
in what I guess we call a memory
but what seems more like a fold in time
because suddenly
today
abuts against

that day we collected coal all along the railroad tracks
and you convinced me to leap from one railroad car to another,
against that day we walked out to the blinds on the Agassiz refuge
and I wore that duck hunting cap that was just like yours,
against that day we climbed into that old potato house,
that day we slid down the sides of those huge raised oil drums,
that day we first rode down Jaeger's hill,
and against that boundless year when we ran as fast as we could
  through Grandma's woods.
And when time retracts itself that way,
I am still running until my throat is raw,
still daring—just barely daring—to cross that river
on the path of rocks and fallen rotten logs,
still crying in fear when I reach the top of that maple tree
  because I know my legs won't carry me back down
  and I'll have to sleep up here
  and the bats will come and get tangled in my hair,
and I hear you coaxing me back then
but it seems like today
and I think I see you
in that bank of trees at the top of the hill
giving me a hand signal that it's okay to come on up
motioning me to follow you,
and I look around just once to see if anyone is watching
and then I run into that past
where I know I will find my future too.

IV

Road Show

"Native Americans" vs. "The Poets"

(some thoughts I had while reading Poetry East)

You know that solitary Indian
sitting in his fringed leathers
on his horse at the rise of the hill
face painted, holding a lance
there just at the horizon?
That guy's got a Ph.D.
He's *the* Indian for Mankato State or Carroll College

Indian professors at universities throughout the country
Exhibit A,
No B, no C, just solitary romanticized A
Not much of a threat that way

Real trouble is
America
still doesn't know what to do with Indians

Looked for your books lately in Powell's
or 57th St. Books?
Check first in folklore or anthropology
Found Louis' *Wolfsong* in black literature
Hell no wonder we all got an identity crisis

You a poet?
No, I just write Indian stuff.

Downwinders

I heard you say "We all live downwind and downstream"
and that sounded right and even profound,
Only later when I learned
that some of us have been selected for fallout,
designated downwinders,
it reminded me of that other profound saying
about how in this land of equal rights and equal justice
"Some of us are more equal than others"

I remember being called from classes in high school
going to the little trailer in the parking lot—
the dentist office for all the Indian kids
I remember one year they used a kind of prong
an electrical shock instead of novocain for numbing
which turned out to be somebody's experiment
I go for my annual visit (a real dentist office now)
my palms sweat with a memory, a terror
that only fellow guinea pigs can know

I think of the Bikini natives
whose home was destroyed by somebody's experiment
of the prisoners and the elders
who became ill from exposure to radioactive materials
in somebody's experiment
of this earth whose insides have been ruptured and contaminated
this earth become like some leper
from somebody's experiment

I think of all the Indian people whose land was first taken,
who live on remnants,

remnants later drained dry of water and oil,
ripped open in searches for its gold heart,
its copper bosom,
its coal black eyes,
remnants chosen for test sites, weapons plants, nuclear burial

I think of my homeland
my family and my people
whose lives are not fashioned in concrete or plastic
We eat together the rice that is gathered from the lakes
we drink tea sweetened with the sap of the maple tree
and I wonder if the poisoning of our foods is
somebody's experiment

I think of the watch makers of Elgin
licking the tips of their brushes
as they painted the radium dials of clocks
poisoning the tongues they needed to speak
so that the time of man might glow in the dark
voiceless now they watch helplessly that time tick by

American Indian Voices: I Wonder If This Is An Indian Poem

So anyway, you say you want to write Indian poems.
Some folks–lots of folks who should know, too,
  will tell you they should talk about things like Indian ceremonies,
  animals and the land,
  the reservation,
  the old time Indian folks.
And maybe about the bad things that have happened to Indian people
    like   and boarding schools and
         removal   relocation.
And now days about Indian drinking,
  and poverty,
  and fetal alcohol syndrome.
They shouldn't have much to do with clock time
  and more to do with spiritual things than with religion.
And you might want to put in some Indian words, too–if you
    know any.
I bet a lot of folks–lots of Indians, too,
  would like the poems pretty much
    and publish them
    and read them
      and talk about them in Minority Literature Classes.
So that's one thing you could do I guess.

But I think a better thing would be just to write about
  the things you know deep down
  and think about a lot
  like the memories and sounds and smells and people and places
  that never leave you even when you sleep

Cuz those are the poems life has written in your soul.
And it doesn't matter if you don't say any stuff in them
  that Indian experts would recognize
  cuz even though us Indians have never been experts on ourselves
  we've done pretty good at finding one another haven't we
  −even when we're all far from home?

Indian Voices have the deep down sound of Indian people
  whether they are writing about catching fish or catching the bus.
When Brenda talks about an auction in Iowa, it sounds very
    Indian to me
  not because an auction is an Indian thing, but cuz she is
  and that's how she sees it.
She talks about families and quilts and good homemade food
  and it makes me want to go there, too,
  same as when she talks about the Red Lake pow-wow.
Yeah, Indian voices do talk about a lot of Indian stuff
  like ricing and fry bread and bingo,
But they talk about computers and car pooling, too.
Indian experts might write a lot about Indians;
Indian voices just write Indian.

Dear Mr. Andy Rooney,

This letter is about mothers and grandmothers
and the things they taught us
and whether we listened.
Remember what your mother said
about always wearing clean underwear?
I hope you take heed
because you, Mr. Rooney
are an accident waiting to happen.
You should take extra care
because you seem to have a way, Mr. Rooney
of fouling a lot of things.
Remember what you said about Blacks awhile back?
You never did really clean that mess up did you?
Oh, you said you had been a supporter
of civil rights in the past,
but you never said you were sorry
for your ignorant offensive remarks.
Was that how your mother
taught you
to make an apology, Mr. Rooney?
And now there's this new mess you have made
of Indian history and Indian issues.
I know a lot of phrases
I'd like to use in this letter to you
to tell you what I think of the things
you said about Indians
and just how wrong you are
and how very ignorant
you revealed yourself to be,

but those phrases all contain words
of which my mother and grandmothers would disapprove.
And I always try to listen to my mothers and grandmothers.

And so I will just ask you
one or two things, Mr. Rooney.
You said there are no great Indian novels,
no poetry, no music, no art,
and I wondered, Mr. Rooney,
do you read? can you hear? can you see?
I was taught by my mother that
I should not judge another
until I understand them well
and so I thought perhaps I
ought to find out about your limitations
and I thought they might explain to me why
you have never heard of N. Scott Momaday
the Kiowa Indian who won the pulitzer prize
for his novel in 1969
and why you have not heard of any of the other
great Native American writers and artists and musicians
like Simon Ortiz and Leslie Silko and James Welch and Louise
    Erdrich
and Buffy St. Marie and Allan Houser and David Bradley and
    R. C. Gorman
and I thought that maybe something has kept you
from realizing how great an influence all the Indian arts
have had on those of the greater America
and how they are even more honored in Europe
where the people don't get the art mixed up
with guilt and land claims.

And then there was this other question
I wanted to ask you, Mr. Rooney
about your idea that our Indian lifestyle is an anachronism.
Don't worry I teach at a university

and I know my English pretty well, Mr. Rooney
and so I know what that word means, too.
You say "the time for the way the Indians lived
is gone. . . and they refuse to accept it."
But it seems to me that what you have said
could not be farther from the truth
and that if you gave it a little thought
(didn't your mother ever say think before you speak?)
that you would come to the same conclusion, too.
You say that the Indian's genius was for
"living. . . without damaging the ozone layer."
Now it seems to me that such a way of living
is not now, particularly not now out of its proper time,
If anything it is the way that the colonizers have lived
and continue to live that is an anachronism.
The time for the way that *they* have lived
in violation of the wisdom of our mothers and grandmothers
in violation of the sacred balance of this Earth Mother
is gone.
And sadly, Mr. Rooney,
they, like you,
refuse to accept the truth of the planet
the truth that my ancestors knew so well
and that Indian people could still teach
if only you would listen.

And finally, Mr. Rooney,
I have to ask you about the history you learned.
My grandmother told me that what I learned in school
was his-story, the story of the "Great White Father,"
the history of the conqueror.
And I wonder if in your many years of life
no one and nothing has ever taught you
about the way that history is constructed
and why.

You write about Indians surrounding the wagon trains
shooting flaming arrows into stagecoaches
carrying off the new schoolmarm.
If these are the only stories from history you know
then perhaps that explains best
the rest of what you have said.
You say that "there have been many efforts
to assimilate the Indian into our society"
but do you know the stories of those efforts, Mr. Rooney
and the price that was paid in human lives and human dignity?
Do you know anything at all about the reservation system,
relocation, allotment, and BIA boarding schools?
If you did, Mr. Rooney, then you would understand
why it is true as you have said,
the one true statement I found in what you wrote,
that "Indians don't want any part of it."

Road Show

for Gordy

White Earth Land Recovery Project
  takin' a bunch of Shinabes on the road,
I worry.
Road show of Kenneth Lincoln's "now day indi'ns"
Me too much or too little of what they want.
I know my edges will not match the master template.

Driving myself down Franklin to Montanito's,
Stop off at an Indian store, named something like Big Bear's,
Look around, buy a pair of earrings, talk to the clerks,
Ask if I'm going the right way to get to Montanito's.
"Hell yes," they say. "Hey maybe we'll close up and come with you."
"Do they have good food?"
"No, pull tabs."
I worry.

Waiting at Montanito's I'm mistaken twice for a regular,
  get a warm, nearly toothless smile from someone else's
    grandmother,
  get a kiss from behind by somebody else's boot-clad hero,
  but both abandon the impostor when they spot the authentic at
    the bar.
Wonder if this is some kind of omen:
To be taken for a regular at a bar on Franklin Avenue.
Worse, to be abandoned at a bar on Franklin Avenue.
Lose some money at pull tabs just to pass the time.
After the meeting, still on edge, I make four wrong turns
  before I find my way
I no longer worry, just expect the worst.

But unaccountably things start to pick up.
Listening to your voice, straining to hear the part
  where the guy talks to the bird
  and asks how far it is to Mexico,
I feel okay. Know we are not some wild west show.
I hope you don't mind my saying, but that little tear
  in your jacket
  just behind your shoulder,
  that made me feel pretty okay
  and not so worried about what people thought
  we were supposed to be.
I liked the fresh air that little tear let in.
I'll try sometime to wear one for you.

Waking to Dreams

Just married mornings over the perking of my coffee
  and the crunching of your cereal,
I recite my dreams to you.
Sometimes you listen,
  always you wonder why
Night adventures move me so
  in waking.
I don't tell you much that first year
  that might make you think I am unstable
I just say I believe in things.

We go to Roberta's poetry reading
  during the second year
She tells the role of dreams
  in her life and her family
And I feel she has explained
  me some to you.
You hear me talk about dreams
  long-distance to my parents
And find it amusing
  but not so odd anymore.
I tell you the crazy marriage
  I dreamed that came true, too.

Then one night last winter
  I wake
  too fully to sleep again.
I tell you later that
  two states away
  my parents rose, too

and my brother
drove to work before five a.m.
I tell you stories of dreams
that have crossed more than miles
And you listen
and sometimes you tell me your dreams, too.

When we visit Bill at Twin Lakes
I ask about the tree that is gone.
"Ahh," he says, "I dreamed it fell on the trailer
and so I cut it down."
I look over at you and nod
Knowing even as we all laugh
that now you believe in some things, too.

V

Sewing Memories

Rewriting your life

not just the part
that matters the most,

but those haunting scenes
that make anger and panic rise in your throat
at the domestic quarrels of strangers.
The same sort
that make my pulse pound in my ears
to drown out that saccharine alcohol voice
of the women two booths away.

Erasing, replacing
the longings that arose from want
the causes
of your jacket fetish
the causes
of the bathtub in my parents' yard
the causes
of all old patterns stumbling on to renew themselves
of personal quirks
and other small tortures.

The children we were
we are.

I've added
a child with chink eyes
to those
bruised souls
whose lives
I rewrite

on my bluest days
and in the midst of my happiest moments
some part that seems physical
surges
with a longing
to repair
the past.

The aches in our bones are memories I'm told.
The tearing and stitching of our flesh
not the physical wear of age
really small but impossible hopes
dreamed endlessly
in smoke-filled pool halls
in one-room cold-water flats
dreams of grease splattered arms
taking shorthand
legs crossed at the ankles
just above a pair of black patent leather pumps.

The little tug in our voices
we wash down with complimentary water
at public podiums and in banquet halls
it is the pull of the small store of joy
of a people born poor
studying in school to be ashamed
it is the shiny marbles
our children shot across muddy school yards
and then washed and lined neatly to dry
it is fresh winter snow served with cream and sugar
nickel tent movies
and hurrah for the fourth of july!

It is your memories too now
that raise the flesh on my arms and legs.
And perhaps in time we can write across

70

that other life with this one,
but never enough to obscure it
just enough to make a new pattern
a new design
pitifully inadequate perhaps
for all that has happened –
but beautiful as only loved pain can be.

And so I write across your life that way
with mine
I write across your life with love
that comes from my own pain
and then, of course,
I write your face across my pain.

Sewing Memories: This Poem I've Wanted to Write

You know there's this poem I've wanted to write
 about sewing
And it has stories in it
 like about the time
 I sewed the sleeves in my dress upside-down
 so the elbow darts lay across the vein on my inner arm
Or about the time you applied for that job
 at the sewing factory
 and came home embarrassed and laughing at yourself
 because you kept answering all the questions on the application
 the same way
 saying how you love to sew
Or about the time you sewed the prom dress for me
 and followed a store-bought pattern
 only to discover that I wasn't exactly made
 like the model for that pattern
 I still remember the shock we had
 when I tried on that dress
 and the upper half of my breasts
 remained uncovered by the blue material
 I always like the story you tell
 about how my date made you pin on my corsage
 and I can remember the looks I drew that night
 I guess they were probably lustful
 but I could only think about how funny the whole thing was
 and how it was even funnier when we remembered

that other story about how when I was ten years old or so
and playing with one of my girlfriends
in the hot hot summer
and we were both wearing long sleeve sweaters over our
    summer tops
because we didn't want the boys to see our arms
and I thought well I guess they still can't see my arms
(because the dress had long sleeves)

This poem also has other sewing stories in it
Like about the time the farm burned down
  when you were a senior in high school
  and all your things burnt up
  and Mum made you that one skirt to wear to school
  out of a pair of old pants that were saved
Or the story you never told me for such a long time
  that makes me mad just to think of it
  about you trying to learn how to sew in home-ec class
  on an electric sewing machine
  when all you had ever used was a pedal machine
  and being teased instead of helped
  even by the teacher

Then there are other sewing things too
  that aren't really stories
  but just these kind of puffs of memory
  that open up big spaces in my present life
  by bursting in whole all at once
  like the puffs of air the doctor shoots against your open eye
  they arrive that way in a quick burst
  so that I feel their weight inside of me
  not a heaviness but just a presence
  that seems to rub against my insides
  the way some animals rub against you to remind you they are
    there
  to remind you they need your attention, too

I remember Grandma mumbling to herself
and hiding her church-forbidden playing cards
when she thought no one was looking
in one of the little drawers of her sewing machine cabinet
the one with the thread spool for a handle
hiding them with the buttons and rickrack and scribbled notes
that had collected there through the years
I remember losing track of time as I studied the crazy quilt
in one of the bedrooms in the old part of the house
trying to find pieces of fabric I could match
with whole things that had been made from the same cloth
And I rather think I'm doing the same thing now

So finally today I think to myself about
how you used to make your own patterns
drawing them carefully, cutting them out of newspaper
How we used to plot to find ways to use flawed material
that we could get on sale
Or looked expectantly through dimestore bundles
always finding that one not-too-ugly for imagining
roll of cloth that became curtains or pajamas
I remember the patched corner of the first quilt I ever made
the yellow and print squares all perfect
but for that single one
the corner I folded under
whenever I wrapped my cry-baby doll
I still like to see her all cozy where she lies
among the other dusty treasures
Do you remember
how Debbie's grandmother used to think I had strange ideas
about sewing
like the time I ran the stripes in the yoke of a top vertically
while in the rest of the top I ran them horizontally
Or the times I made that flocked drindle skirt
that red white and blue fuzzy pillow

74

Into all those things we made
we sewed bits of our bodies
and bits of our dreams
we stitched in errors more bold
than those required in sand paintings
And what we created seemed truly to be ours
because we did them that way
filled with make-believe and mistakes
instead of the usual way
and maybe this poem about sewing
refused to come out for such a long time
because I was trying to follow someone else's perfect pattern
So I thought I'd just make it our way
lay the memories and stories out
zig-zag through time
and stitch them together the way I see them

II.

I remember you sewing away your loneliness
days when we were at school
and Daddy was in Montana working construction
I remember all the Barbie Doll clothes you made
for my dolls and to sell for extra money
I still see the little buckskin dresses
the tiny fur jackets
hanging in the window of the Model Meat Market
I remember the matching outfits you sewed
for Robert and I
especially the sailor suits because we have those in that picture
Others I remember because there was so much of you in them
like that pink and white gingham dress you made for me
and decorated all across the hem with black cross-stitching
I remember my lucky dress with the covered buttons
The jean jacket and matching purse you made

75

that I didn't wear very much because I thought I looked too fat
I still have that purse (and maybe the jacket, too)
I never could let it go because I have never really felt finished
    with it
Actually I have a lot of things you've sewed for me
  packed away somewhere
I don't need them to remember
  but they are like the books in my library
  I may never have the time to read them again
  because I have so many books I haven't yet read at all
  but their covers remind me
  of the stories in the pages
  of the time I read them and how they made me feel
  of the richness of my life
  so filled with all these stories

When we moved into this house
  and I unpacked
  I put on many of those stories of my past
  and remembered you with love
  and all our times
  of happiness and of sadness
  and found them all to have their own beauty
  just as these pieces of time
  all multi-colored and mismatched fashion
  tell their own stories
  of life lived in loss and in longing
  and yet in fulfillment, too
  of a kind we had not known of
  and though we cry and fear what is to come
  we have this love of odd design
  that shields us as a garment
  and we hold tightly together
  and thus care less and less each year
  that what we have constructed or sown with our lives

may not be perfect
for the blemishes and errors
we tried to hide in the corners
make that love more dear
for not having given at the seams

All of these things I feel in that one air burst of memory
that comes as I unfold the stories
shake off the dust
hold them out in front of me
or gaze at them across my body in a full-length mirror
I feel their age upon me and count their years
and yet I know too
how young these stories are
and how they will live
whether or not I save
the pieces of cloth
into which we sewed the stories
Suddenly I feel my own insignificance
and hurry to put them gently back
so as not to disturb too much
the power they have accumulated

One of the best things about the threads of this sewing
is that they keep pulling in more
more people, more years, more colors of events
and the stitches can attach all the things of memory
not just flat and smooth pieces of cloth
but bits of fur added for design
a fringe at the bottom instead of a hem
ribbons of all colors and fabrics
even the jingles like on the dance dresses
the smell of pine sap that never really washes away
but sinks into fabrics
and lingers forever like the sweetgrass smell of baskets
the taste and heaviness of leather

the swish of corduroy rubbing together on my legs
the filmy seduction of sheers and lace
the colors and patterns of beads
all things sewn together
so much like memories
stitched sometimes in hidden seams
sometimes boldly patched together
with unmatched fabrics and unmatched threads
knowing that sometimes usefulness
counts more than beauty
And when I see the tiny patchworks
  hung in country galleries
  captioned and bartered for
  I know we have this masterpiece
  too big to hang on any wall
  and that we've spared no expense
  but I wonder what the world would think
  to see that pair of narrow, oh way too narrow green tweed
  crooked-legged pants hanging on a peg above my couch
  and what would be the bid I wonder
  on that 4-H inspired red-and-white-checkered tablecloth
  that has unraveled itself down to the size of a diaper

The gallery of my sewing memories is full
  of you at embroidery
  you stitching birch bark
  Aunt Ida making rugs with her half blind eyes
  my homemade elf, my mouse, and all my bedroom rabbits
I remember the scent of hot rubber
  the scent of that old sewing machine begging for a rest
I remember you kneeling on the grass
  threading that long curved needle
  then leaning inside to stitch the seat of that ancient red Buick
I was sure then that with a big enough needle
  you could pull just about anything together

But the passing of time has proved me wrong
and I've come to realize
that you didn't need that needle
at all

Asphalt, the Odd Perfume of Summer

July heat has me moist as some packaged airline towlette –
    but warm.
Drive windows down for the breeze.
And then: "Road Construction Next 15 Miles."
Slow the car and the air stops brushing by me,
Hangs heavy, pressing against my face, my throat, my chest
Breathing means tasting and swallowing the heat
And now the thick oily smell.
I get the stop flag and sit watching the machinery,
    the men tanned deeply and looking somehow fresh
    in the heat, fresh beneath layers of dirt and calluses,
    looking like you leaving before six in the morning,
    like you coming home twelve hours later,
    like you throwing horse-shoes after supper.
Heat becomes visible waves, rhythmic waves breaking
    against the shores of time, lapping, wearing away
    the barriers, waves rushing forward, receding backward,
    washing against, mingling the sands of memory;
    riding the waves, you come.
I wait for you at the curb, or on the steps,
I ride my blue bike, the one you hid for a surprise,
the one I knew was not for me because I didn't know how to ride,
I ride my feet against the wood blocks you added to help me reach
the peddles.
Round the yard, listening for the sound of your dump truck.
I wait and you come
    smelling of asphalt and perspiration
    carrying your red water jug and black lunch box
    swooping me up

rubbing my face a little with your whiskers
passing with your kiss a peppermint lifesaver warm from your mouth.
The go flag is out, and I'm waved on.
I drive while I open the lunch box,
   while I remember the mingled smells there
               of pickles, summer sausage and soggy cookies,
   while I search through the wrappers
               for that gumdrop or tootsie roll you have left for me.
The flagman on the other side waves as I pass,
   and in his hand I see yours
   yours cut and bruised, dotted with iodine
   your large hands working the tiny buttons
      tying decades of bows at the backs of my dresses.
Driving through the heat, I feel the pressure of your hand
   on my shoulder blade as we enter a building,
   on my knee as you tickle me,
The pressure of your hand as it covers mine while we sit at the
kitchen table and talk of the times when like the summer flowers
we never tired of reciting the same line – "Morning glory, think
it will reindeer" – when our lives were filled with the hot
endless days of summer, filled with Sunday watermelon and frilly
dresses, and the times when you came fresh from your job at
Asphalt Paving Company.

Day Moon

for Andy

Spent last night hearing Indian voices
Telling disjointed stories, sending laughter into the dark,
Things began to feel familiar
Thought we should have a kerosene lantern
   a deck of cards
   and an oilcloth covering the table,
Thought someone should have said "Howwah!"
   or told a Star Bad Boy story.
I began to see someone on the edge of the circle
   squeezing a tennis ball over and over
In the shadow someone stood by the water pail
   drinking from the dipper
The dogs outside were barking
   and the cold was creeping in by the windows and doors
I know someone got up to feed the fire
   but they never came back
Because suddenly everyone was moving
   pushing their chairs back
   standing up from the table
We walked through long halls to the elevator
   got off at separate floors and found our rooms
   closed ourselves in and hoped for dreams
   to keep us company.

Today I wake up sick, my back sore
   I don't go down for breakfast
   decide not to take the bus to the conference

Later in the morning I drive out
  wondering what will be left of the night's magic
Looking at the sky I see my answer—
A day moon, an omen I think
  of the mingling, the trespassing of logic's boundaries
Not just the dissolving of divisions of time,
  but the melting together of lives.

We sit around the banquet table
  polite public distance maintained
But I see us all lying crosswise in a single bed
  becoming tangled in our sleep
  waking to wrestle playfully for control of the quilt
And when they call your name
  and you go up to receive your prize
I see Danielle walking and Gordy and Patrick
I see Denise pause by the mike, then me, then you
I see Diane and Lupe shaking hands and blushing
  even though they are not here

When we all come back and sit down again
Someone has switched the table
It's corners are rounded out
Now we sit squeezed together, bumping knees and elbows,
  stepping on each other's toes
Elation has made us giddy with plans
  for the future, or is it the past?
The moon shown that day when we won something
  we were all afraid we had lost.

Certificate of Live Birth:
Escape From the Third Dimension

(Quotations taken from Banesh Hoffman's introduction to Flatland: A
Romance of Many Dimensions *written by Edwin A. Abbott.)*

"We do indeed have four dimensions. But even in relativity,
they are not all of the same sort. Only three are spatial. The
fourth is temporal; and we are unable to move freely in time.
We cannot return to days gone by, nor avoid the coming of
tomorrow. We can neither hasten nor retard our journey into
the future."

I.

Shuffling papers
    rushing to find some critical
    form or letter or journal
    mired amid the stacks that have collected
    that I've hidden in every corner of the room

Tiny new-born footprints step out of flatland
    a xerox copy of my birth certificate
Nostalgia
    no time—
Yet as I hold the single sheet
    it shapes itself and curves out of my hand

Chubby ankle circled firmly
    protesting kicking held still
    foot inked
    the page indelibly marked
    with my unwilling signature

Perhaps some memory of that first helplessness
   makes me struggle still against capture
   against hint of bonds—
You won't imprint me again

_____

   "Our fourth dimension, time, true dimension though it be, does
   not permit us to escape from a three-dimensional prison. It does
   enable us to get out, for if we wait patiently for time to pass, our
   sentence will be served and we shall be set free. That is hardly an
   escape, however. To escape we must travel through time to some
   moment when the prison is wide open, or in ruins, or not yet
   built; and then, having stepped outside, we must reverse the
   direction of our time travel to return to the present."

II.

Or perhaps it was your capture
   that so enraged my yet unconscious mind
   that brought me kicking into the world
For yours was the more torturous:
   Father, caucasian.
   Mother, caucasian.
What pain what shame what fear
   must have forced that check in that flatland box?

Mother, should I correct it?

But no it is more accurate
   just as it stands
In that mark I read your life
I read the history of Indian people in this country
It is my heritage more truly than any account of bloodlines
It tells the story of a people's capture
It tells the story of a people's struggle to survive

And, Mother, this poem is the certificate of our live birth
For together we have escaped their capture
Our time together outdistances their prison
It "stands in ruins" within the circle of our lives:
  Father, caucasian.
  Mother, American Indian.
  Daughter, mixedblood.

Kimberly M. Blaeser, of Anishinaabe and German ancestry, is an enrolled member of the Minnesota Chippewa Tribe and grew up on White Earth Reservation in Northwestern Minnesota. She is an Assistant Professor in English and Comparative Literature at the University of Wisconsin-Milwaukee where she teaches twentieth century American literature, specializing in Native American Literature and American Nature Writing. She currently lives on six and a half acres of woods and wetlands in rural Lyons township in Wisconsin.

Her work which includes poetry, personal essays, short fiction, journalism, and scholarly articles, has appeared in numerous Canadian and American journals and collections including: *Earth Song, Sky Spirit, The Colour of Resistance, New Voices in Native American Literary Criticism, Looking at the Words of Our People, Narrative Chance: Postmodern Discourse on Native American Indian Literatures, Nebraska English Journal, Akwe-kon, Cream City Review, World Literature Today* and *Gatherings*. Blaeser's study of a fellow White Earth writer, *Gerald Vizenor: Writing in the Oral Tradition* will be published by the University of Oklahoma Press.

Blaeser says of her writing: "In both my creative and scholarly work I hope to explore the way writing can cross the boundaries of print, seeking not to report but to engender life, seeking to understand and enact the ways of survival."

Statement by the Artist and Picturemaker

I carry in my genes ancient memories. Memories of my Grandfather's Grandfather who led Karl Bodmer, an artist from Germany, up the Missouri River to document the tribal customs and ethnology of the North American Indians. Memories of my Grandmother's Grandmother, a full blood Assiniboine Indian, who married my ancestor from Ireland.

Memories of Fort Laramie where my ancestor, David Dawson Mitchell brought the largest gathering of the Plains tribes ever in recorded history. A peacemaking venture that was undermined by Congress.

Memories of my Great Great Aunt, Jenny Firemoon, a healer woman who prepared a meal for Sitting Bull.

Recorded in my genes are the smells of Sage and burning Sweetgrass on the Montana prairies. And Wolf Point, the early settlement on the banks of the Missouri River; the birthplace of my Father and Grandfather, Charlie Mitchell, whose bones are buried on a fenceless hill next to "Redfish", a noted leader and warrior.

My paintings are expressions of feelings, like the unexplained sadness of a quiet meadow in October, the mysterious benediction when in the presence of ancient trees, or the excitement of a dancer whirling with the intensity and timing of the drums.

For me as a picturemaker, my concerns are not to just portray surface imagery, which doesn't last, but to explore and journey with the viewer evoking questions from an ancestral or primitive place that only he or she can answer.

Charles Mitchell